EARTH'S CRUST

To Conor...

Respect our planet!

BY CONRAD J. STORAD

Conrad Storad

2012

♡Reading

LERNER PUBLICATIONS COMPANY • MINNEAPOLIS

For my dad and mom. Thanks for showing me the wonderful world of books and reading!

The photographs in this book are used with the permission of: U.S. Geological Survey Photo Library, pp. 1, 1 (title type), 4, 6 (background), 12, 16, 18 (background), 24 (background), 29, 30, 31, 36, 37, 38 (background), 44 (background), 45 (background), 46, 46 (background), 47 (background); © Paul van Gaalen/zefa/CORBIS, p. 5; © Adam Jones/Visuals Unlimited, p. 6; U.S. Fish and Wildlife Service, p. 7; © National Park Service, pp. 8, 26, 28, 47; NASA, p. 10; © Paul A. Souders/CORBIS, p. 11; © Sam Lund/Independent Picture Service, p. 13; © Todd Strand/Independent Picture Service, p. 14; © Layne Kennedy/CORBIS, p. 15; PhotoDisc Royalty Free by Getty Images, pp. 18, 34; © Jason Hawkes/CORBIS, p. 20; © Altitude/Peter Arnold, Inc., p. 21; © Tom Van Sant/CORBIS, p. 22; © Tim Hauf/Visuals Unlimited, p. 24; © Science VU/NASA/Visuals Unlimited, p. 25; © Galen Rowell/CORBIS, p. 27; Captain Budd Christman, NOAA Corps, p. 33; © Roger Ressmeyer/CORBIS, p. 35; © John R. Kreul/Independent Picture Service, p. 38; © Amos Nachoum/CORBIS, p. 39; NOAA/NGDC, p. 41; OAR/National Undersea Research Program, p. 42; © Peter Adams/zefa/CORBIS, p. 43; © James L. Amos/ CORBIS, p. 48 (top); U.S. Department of Interior, U.S. Geological Survey, p. 48 (bottom).

Front cover: © National Park Service.
Front cover title type: U.S. Geological Survey Photo Library.
Back cover: © Reuters/CORBIS.

Illustrations on pp. 9, 17, 19, 23, 32, 40 by Laura Westlund, copyright © by Lerner Publications Company.

Text copyright © 2007 by Conrad J. Storad

Lerner Publications Company
A division of Lerner Publishing Group, Inc.
241 First Avenue North
Minneapolis, MN 55401 U.S.A

Website address: www.lernerbooks.com

Library of Congress Cataloging-in-Publication Data

Storad, Conrad J.
    Earth's Crust / by Conrad J. Storad.
        p.   cm. — (Early bird earth science)
    Includes index.
    ISBN-13: 978–0–8225-5944–3 (lib. bdg. : alk. paper)
    ISBN-10: 0-8225-5944-7 (lib. bdg. : alk. paper)
    1. Earth—Crust —Juvenile literature. 2. Earth—Surface—Juvenile literature. I. Title. II. Series.
QE511.S724 2007
551.1'3—dc22   2005016423

Manufactured in the United States of America
2 3 4 5 6 7 – JR – 12 11 10 09 08 07

CONTENTS

BE A WORD DETECTIVE

Can you find these words as you read about Earth's crust?
Be a detective and try to figure out what they mean. You
can turn to the glossary on page 46 for help.

core	geologists	mid-ocean ridges
crust	lava	mountains
earthquake	magma	plates
erupts	magma chamber	rift
faults	mantle	volcanoes

Earth's crust is always under you. But most of the time you can't see it. Why can't you see the crust?

CHAPTER 1
PLANET PARTS

Take a walk outside. Now look down at your feet. You may be standing on grass or dirt. Or maybe you're standing on concrete or blacktop. You also are standing on Earth's crust.

In most places, the crust is hidden. It may be covered by grass, cornfields, or forests. Or it may be covered by the water in rivers, lakes, or oceans.

In many places, plants and soil cover Earth's crust.

But in some places, you can see Earth's crust. Rocky cliffs near the seashore are part of the crust. So are the steep walls of deep canyons.

The crust is a layer of rock that covers our planet. Under the oceans, the crust is about 3 miles thick. Under the land, the crust is much thicker. Below your feet, the crust goes down as deep as 40 miles! A car driving on a highway takes more than half an hour to go that far.

Part of Earth's crust can be seen in this desert in Colorado.

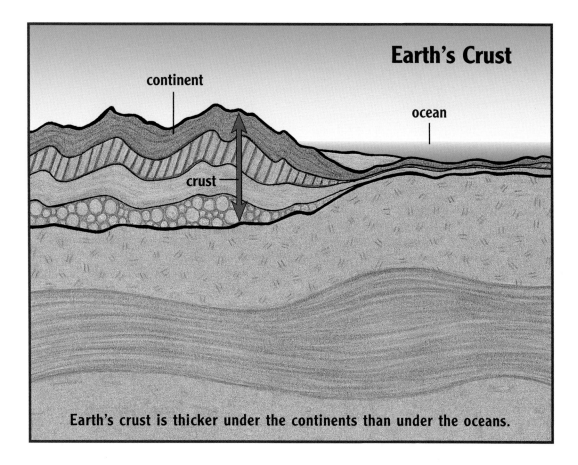

Earth's Crust

continent

ocean

crust

Earth's crust is thicker under the continents than under the oceans.

It might sound like Earth's crust is really thick. But compared to the whole planet, the crust is actually very thin. Imagine that you could shrink Earth and make it the size of a basketball. Then Earth's crust would be thinner than this book. The tallest mountains would be specks too small to see.

This is what Earth looks like to astronauts in space.

Now imagine you are an astronaut flying more than 100 miles above Earth. Earth looks like a beautiful, giant, blue ball spinning below you. It is surrounded by a layer of air with thick, swirling white clouds. That layer is called the atmosphere (AT-muhs-feer). Below the atmosphere, you see big chunks of brown and green. Those chunks are huge pieces of land called continents. And you see huge patches of blue water. Those patches are the oceans. Most of Earth is covered by oceans.

Most of Earth is covered by oceans.

But what does Earth look like inside? If you could slice the planet in half, you could see all of its parts. You would see other layers under the crust. Of course, you can't really slice Earth in half. So how do we know about the layers? Geologists (jee-AHL-uh-jists) tell us. Geologists are scientists who study Earth.

These people are geologists. They are studying rocks near a volcano.

Like Earth, a hard-boiled egg has three main layers. An egg's layers are the shell, the white, and the yolk.

Geologists use special tools to study Earth's parts. They use hammers, picks, and shovels. They also use computers, microscopes, and other tools. Geologists study all of Earth's layers. They study how the layers formed. They also study how the parts of our planet work. Some geologists say Earth's layers are like the parts of a giant hard-boiled egg. Let's whack open that egg and look inside.

Earth's crust is kind of like the egg's hard outside shell. It is a thin layer on the outside of the planet. Most of the crust is made of two kinds of rock called granite (GRAN-iht) and basalt (buh-SAHLT). Under the continents, the crust is mostly made of granite. Under the oceans, the crust is mostly made of basalt.

Granite rock comes in many different colors. It is often used to make buildings.

Basalt is usually dark gray. When basalt breaks, the pieces have flat, smooth sides.

Below the crust is a very thick layer of rock. This layer is called the mantle. The mantle is more than 1,800 miles thick. It is like the springy, white part of the hard-boiled egg. Most of the rock in the mantle is always moving. But it moves very slowly, kind of like toothpaste being squeezed from a tube.

The mantle is much hotter than the crust. And the bottom of the mantle is even hotter than the top of the mantle. In some parts of the mantle, rock gets so hot that it melts! Melted rock inside Earth is called magma.

Melted rock glows bright yellow, orange, or red. Its color becomes darker as it cools.

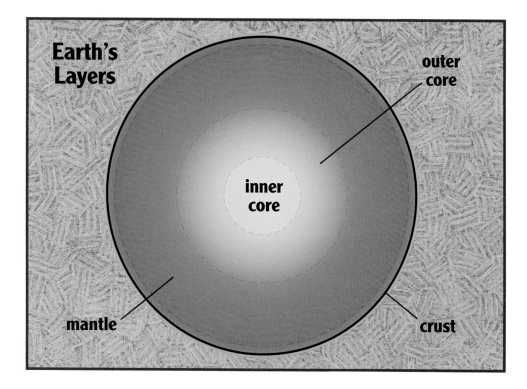

Earth's Layers

outer core

inner core

mantle

crust

At Earth's center is another thick layer. This layer is called the core. The core is sort of like the yellow yolk of the egg. But Earth's core has two parts. The outside part is made of super-hot, melted rock. This part is called the outer core. The outer core is more than 1,300 miles thick. Under the outer core is the inner core. The inner core is made of solid metal. It is more than 1,500 miles thick.

Most of Earth's crust is covered up, so you can't see it. If you could see all of Earth's crust, what would it look like?

CHAPTER 2
MOVING PIECES

Earth's crust is not just one piece, like the shell of an egg. Instead, the crust is cracked into lots of big pieces. The pieces are called plates.

Geologists say that there are seven huge plates and lots of smaller ones. If we could see them, they would look sort of like the pieces of a jigsaw puzzle.

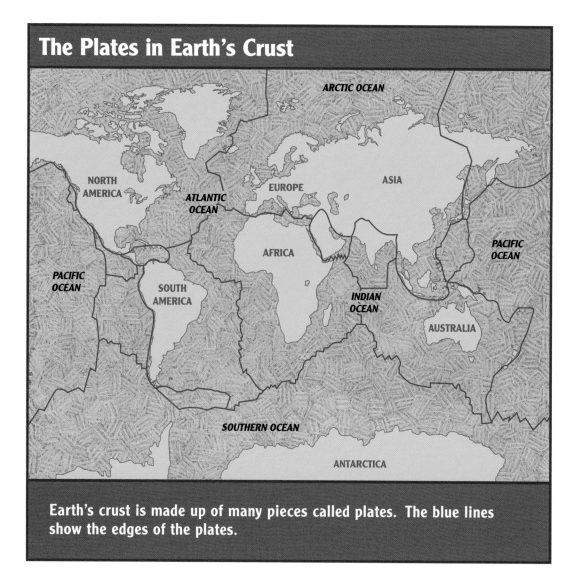

The Plates in Earth's Crust

ARCTIC OCEAN

NORTH AMERICA

EUROPE

ASIA

ATLANTIC OCEAN

PACIFIC OCEAN

AFRICA

PACIFIC OCEAN

SOUTH AMERICA

INDIAN OCEAN

AUSTRALIA

SOUTHERN OCEAN

ANTARCTICA

Earth's crust is made up of many pieces called plates. The blue lines show the edges of the plates.

Most of Earth's plates have both water and land on them.

Most of these big, rocky plates have both land and water on top of them. But some are covered only by oceans.

The big plates float on top of the mantle. They do not stay in one place. Instead, they move very slowly across Earth's surface. They can move a long way. But that takes millions of years.

This place in Africa is called the Great Rift Valley. The valley formed because two of Earth's plates are slowly moving away from each other.

The plates carry the continents and the oceans with them as they move. Look at a globe in your classroom. Can you find North America and Europe on the globe? These two continents are on different plates. North America's plate is moving away from Europe's plate. It is not moving very fast, though. It only moves about 1 inch each year.

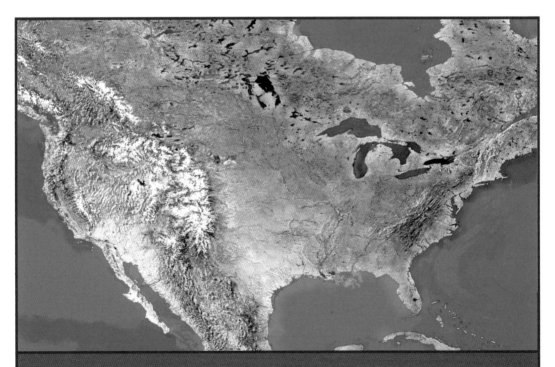

North America is one of Earth's continents. This is what North America looks like from space.

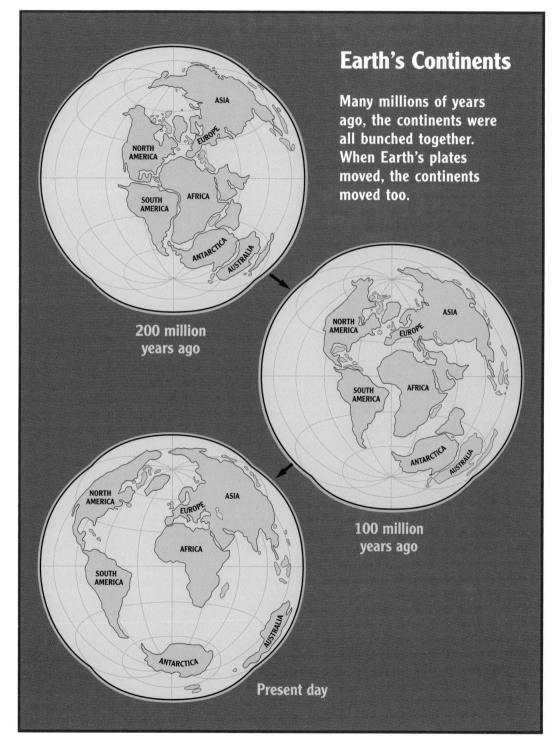

Earth's Continents

Many millions of years ago, the continents were all bunched together. When Earth's plates moved, the continents moved too.

200 million years ago

100 million years ago

Present day

23

Mountains are part of Earth's crust. Why do mountains stick up above the rest of the crust?

CHAPTER 3

MOUNTAINS, CRACKS, AND HOLES

Sometimes Earth's rocky plates push against one another. It is like a giant wreck in super-slow motion. Earth's crust crumples and folds when the big plates smash into one another. Over millions of years, the folded crust is pushed higher and higher. These big folds in the crust are called mountains.

From space, mountains look like wrinkles in the ground.

The Rocky Mountains are a long line of mountains. The northern end of the line is in Alaska. The southern end is in Mexico.

Look at the globe again. Look at the Rocky Mountains in North America. Look at the Andes Mountains in South America. Look at the Himalaya Mountains between India and China. These are some of the tallest mountains in the world. The big plates of Earth's crust are crashing together near these mountains. The crust is folding higher and higher. Very, very slowly, the mountains are growing taller.

Some of the Andes Mountains are so tall that their tops are above the clouds!

The Appalachian Mountains are in the eastern United States. These mountains formed a very long time ago.

Earth's crust may break near the places where the big plates push against each other. Sometimes cracks and holes form in Earth's crust.

Cracks in the crust are called faults. Some faults are deep underground. Other faults can be seen on the surface.

Some of these cracks in the crust are short. But others are very long. The San Andreas Fault in California is one of the most famous cracks in Earth's crust. This fault is more than 700 miles long.

The San Andreas Fault is a very long crack in Earth's crust.

An earthquake made big cracks in this road.

Sometimes pieces of the crust near these giant cracks move. Huge slabs of rock push against one another along a fault. The two slabs try to slide in different directions. The slabs might push against one another for hundreds of years. Finally, one slab slides past the other slab in a short, powerful movement. The movement of the slabs is called an earthquake. During an earthquake, the ground moves. The ground may shake hundreds of miles away from the fault!

The ground under this building moved during an earthquake. The building broke into pieces.

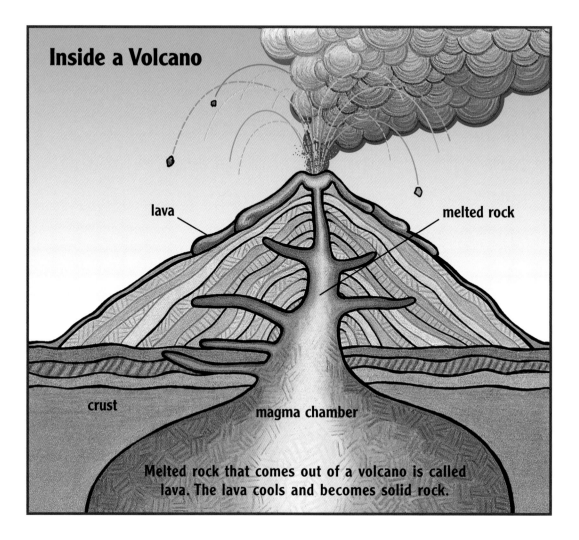

Inside a Volcano

lava

melted rock

crust

magma chamber

Melted rock that comes out of a volcano is called
lava. The lava cools and becomes solid rock.

Holes also form in Earth's crust. These
holes are often close to the edges of the giant
plates. Holes in the crust are called volcanoes.
Beneath a volcano is a huge space filled with
hot magma. The space is called a magma

chamber. Sometimes the hot magma pushes all the way up to the surface. Then the volcano erupts. Melted rock comes out onto Earth's surface. Melted rock that comes out of a volcano is called lava (LAH-vuh).

Most volcanoes erupt for a while, then rest for a while. Over a long time, the cooled lava from a volcano can pile up to make a big mountain.

Some volcanoes erupt slowly. The magma begins to leak upward through the crust. When it gets to the surface, the magma becomes lava. The lava flows slowly across the ground, like a fiery river.

When a volcano erupts, hot lava may flow across the ground.

This bumpy rock is lava that has cooled and hardened.

Some volcanoes spray ash into the air. Ash is bits of rock that are about the same size as marbles.

Other volcanoes erupt very quickly. Under these volcanoes, magma pushes harder and harder against the sides of the magma chamber. Finally, it pushes so hard that the volcano explodes! Big, fiery globs of lava may fly through the air. These globs are called lava bombs. Gas and bits of rock come out of the ground too.

This volcano is spraying hot lava into the air.

When two of Earth's plates collide, the crust may wrinkle to form mountains. What else may happen when plates crash together?

CHAPTER 4
MAKING NEW CRUST

The big, rocky plates of Earth's crust are always moving. They slide past one another. They crash together. Part of one plate may be pushed under another plate. When the edge of a plate is pushed down into the mantle, it melts. But that part of Earth's crust isn't gone forever.

The part of the crust that is under the oceans is very important. This is where new crust is made.

Some volcanoes form under the oceans. After a long time, an underwater volcano may grow tall enough to stick up above the water. Then it is called a volcanic island.

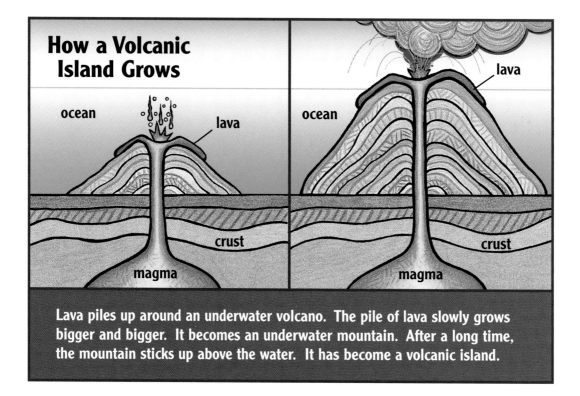

How a Volcanic Island Grows

ocean

lava

crust

magma

ocean

lava

crust

magma

Lava piles up around an underwater volcano. The pile of lava slowly grows bigger and bigger. It becomes an underwater mountain. After a long time, the mountain sticks up above the water. It has become a volcanic island.

Under the oceans, the crust is thin. The mantle is close to the surface. In some places, the mantle pushes up along the cracks between the big plates. The plates bulge upward. These bulges become long ridges. Geologists call them mid-ocean ridges. Mid-ocean ridges are thousands of miles long. One big ridge is in the middle of the Atlantic Ocean. Another is under the Pacific Ocean.

Along the top of each ridge is a deep crack. The crack is called a rift. Magma slowly flows up through the rift. Lava pours out onto the ocean's bottom. The cold ocean water cools the lava, changing it into solid rock. This rock is new crust.

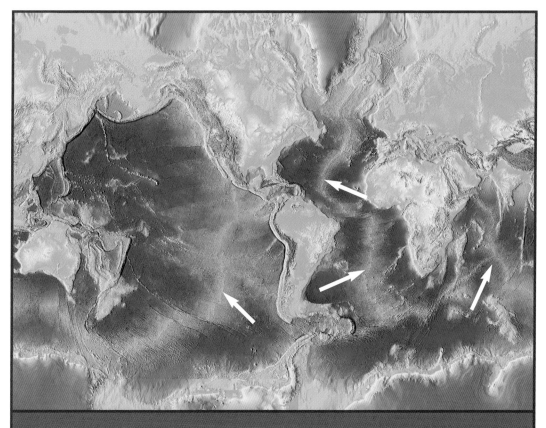

This picture shows Earth's surface from space. The arrows are pointing at ridges where new crust is forming.

Lava pours out of rifts and becomes solid rock. Sometimes the lava cools into huge lumps that are shaped like pillows.

Old crust melts and new crust forms.
Earth's plates move and make mountains grow.
Earth's crust is always changing.

These tall mountains are in Chile, a country in South America.

A NOTE TO ADULTS
ON SHARING A BOOK

When you share a book with a child, you show that reading is important. To get the most out of the experience, read in a comfortable, quiet place. Turn off the television and limit other distractions, such as telephone calls.

Be prepared to start slowly. Take turns reading parts of this book. Stop occasionally and discuss what you're reading. Talk about the photographs. If the child begins to lose interest, stop reading. When you pick up the book again, revisit the parts you have already read.

BE A VOCABULARY DETECTIVE

The word list on page 5 contains words that are important in understanding the topic of this book. Be word detectives and search for the words as you read the book together. Talk about what the words mean and how they are used in the sentence. Do any of these words have more than one meaning? You will find the words defined in a glossary on page 46.

WHAT ABOUT QUESTIONS?

Use questions to make sure the child understands the information in this book. Here are some suggestions:

What did this paragraph tell us? What does this picture show? What do you think we'll learn about next? What are some places where Earth's crust can be seen? What are the names of Earth's layers? What is the difference between magma and lava? What happens when Earth's plates push against one another? How does new crust form under the oceans?

If the child has questions, don't hesitate to respond with questions of your own, such as: What do *you* think? Why? What is it that you don't know? If the child can't remember certain facts, turn to the index.

INTRODUCING THE INDEX

The index helps readers find information without searching through the whole book. Turn to the index on page 47. Choose an entry such as *volcanoes* and ask the child to use the index to find out how a volcanic island forms. Repeat with as many entries as you like. Ask the child to point out the differences between an index and a glossary. (The index helps readers find information, while the glossary tells readers what words mean.)

EARTH

BOOKS

Anderson, Peter. *A Grand Canyon Journey: Tracing Time in Stone.* New York: Franklin Watts, 1997.

Cole, Joanna. *The Magic School Bus: Inside the Earth.* New York: Scholastic Press, 1997.

Hooper, Meredith. *The Pebble in My Pocket: A History of Our Earth.* New York: Viking, 1996.

Redfern, Martin. *The Kingfisher Young People's Book of Planet Earth.* New York: Kingfisher, 1999.

Stamper, Judith. *Voyage to the Volcano.* New York: Scholastic, 2003.

WEBSITES

Earth's Continental Plates
http://www.enchantedlearning.com/subjects/astronomy/planets/earth/Continents.shtml
This site includes an animation that shows how the continents have moved during Earth's history.

Neighborhood Rocks
http://www.saltthesandbox.org/rocks/index.htm
Learn all about rock collecting! This website includes descriptions of some kinds of rocks you might find in your neighborhood.

OLogy: Plates on the Move
http://ology.amnh.org/earth/plates/index.html
Interactive animations let you explore how Earth's plates affect our world.

GLOSSARY

core: Earth's center. The core has two parts called the inner core and the outer core.

crust: Earth's rocky outer layer

earthquake: a movement of parts of Earth's crust that makes the ground shake

erupts: lets melted rock and gases go out onto Earth's surface

faults: cracks in Earth's crust

geologists (jee-AHL-uh-jists): scientists who study Earth

lava (LAH-vuh): melted rock that comes out of a volcano

magma: melted rock inside Earth

magma chamber: a huge space under a volcano. The space is filled with hot melted rock.

mantle: the thick layer of rock under Earth's crust

mid-ocean ridges: places under the ocean where pieces of Earth's crust bulge upward and new crust is formed

mountains: big folds in Earth's crust

plates: huge pieces of Earth's crust

rift: a deep crack

volcanoes: holes in Earth's crust

INDEX

Pages listed in **bold** type refer to photographs.